LET GO

A LITTLE GUIDEBOOK TO FREEDOM

ANTONY S SCANDALE
COPYRIGHT 2015
INNER POWER PUBLISHING

INNER POWER PUBLISHING

INNER POWER PUBLISHING

Copyright © 2015 Antony S Scandale

All rights reserved.

ISBN 978-0-993935 9-0-9

Antony Scandale (the "Author") has written, and Inner Power Publishing (the "Publisher") has published this work in order to provide the reader with one perspective on affirmations and positive behaviour. Although the author and publisher wholeheartedly believe in the views expressed and information conveyed in this book, the Author and Publisher do not assume and hereby disclaim any liability to any party for any loss, damage, or disruption caused as a direct or indirect result of the views and information contained in this book, whether such loss, damage or disruption results from negligence, accident, or any other cause.

Dedicated to my loving mother and father who always provided me with multiple opportunities for a better life. Without their loving support, belief and work ethic, I could never be the person I am today.

ACKNOWLEDGMENTS

I would like to extend my sincere appreciation to my wonderful team who gave me the push in the right direction, most notably, Ina Khan. Without your marketing and coaching prowess, this book would never have been created – and to my sister Angie Scandale, for sacrificing a lot of her precious time and effort into this project. I would also like to give a big thank you to Basim Mirza and Ramsha Ali for their incredible hard work with marketing and copywriting - I am blessed to have you on board.

To Peggy McColl and her assistant Lindsay Boileau for believing in me. Bob Proctor and Sandy Gallagher for providing me with that extra push when I needed it the most. Patti Knoles for her brilliant cover and book design. Sarah Steinerstauch for her love and support and for reminding me to stay focused and positive. Stewart and Janet Swerdlow for helping me expose my true inner self. Renée Elliott for her inspiring words about life and personal success. To Andrew and Nicola Hersant, thank you for your support and help in completing this book.

To all my followers, subscribers and readers - my heartfelt wish is to meet all of you in person. Thank you and keep pushing yourself to do better and to be better. Our world needs you.

I would be remiss to not mention and thank all of my friends and to my extended family near and far who helped shape me as the person you see today.

My brothers Dean and Kevin Scandale, and finally, to my loving mother and father who never stopped supporting my long and arduous journey. I am forever grateful for your patience and unconditional love.

FOREWORD

You hold in your hands a tool of great significance. This book contains an opportunity for anyone who takes the time to read and apply its contents. The invitation is for personal growth, change and expansion. You may ask how can I grow, change and expand when I am letting go of that which has been a part of me all of my life? I can think of nothing more powerful than the decision to let go; to let go of that which no longer serves me.

We often hang on to beliefs, ideas, clothes, memories and habits out of habit. By habit, I imply unconscious behavior. We forget why things are significant yet we keep "things" around out of comfort. This is who we are and we attempt to define ourselves by our past, whether we are aware of it or not. The author has given you a gift. The gift is in the awareness of your power. There is no need to define your-self through or by the past. The opportunity is to define your future now by letting go. Think of this as an exercise in de-cluttering. When we consciously release the old ideas, objects and habits, there is space for the creation of an abundance of more through choice. "More" of whatever it is that you want. The Author is providing you choice!

The word affirmation comes from the Latin 'affirmare' which means to make steady of, to strengthen. Napoleon Hill talks about the concept of Auto Suggestion in his brilliant work "Think and Grow Rich." The concept is that we program our mind through the thoughts we think with both repetition and emotion. In this book, the affirmation is an opportunity to explore a new idea and perhaps to challenge a belief you have which you are not even aware of. The author follows it up immediately with a life relevant application of the new idea. Brilliance!

I encourage you to explore the new ideas and apply them to your life. The ideas may seem simple on the surface yet the ramifications of applying "simple" can be life altering. Internalize the ideas, which you connect with and come back to the book often. You will not be the same person in 30 days and the material here will have added meaning for you at some point. Most importantly, apply the ideas in your life where you see the opportunity NOW. This is not a project to be completed over a weekend; personal growth is a lifelong opportunity for greatness. I see greatness in this book and in you. You see, the truth is Antony can't do the work for you and you can't do it by yourself. The author has provided this work to you as his part in your growth and success. I encourage you to do your part. You will be so happy you took the steps. You will be amazed what awareness and action can do for you. I am excited for your journey!

Edward Wheeler DC

Why Coach

Thinking Into Results Consultant

Professor of International Business and Applied Mind Science

CEO- Vision Rockies

Broomfield, Colorado

PREFACE

My dear friends,

The royal road to a happier lifestyle begins with letting go of the past, and ultimately, it starts with you. It is nearly impossible to enjoy a marvelous, harmonious lifestyle when we are stuck thinking about what happened, or what could have been.

Accept, right now, we are all creatures of habit. Yet understand, habits do not necessarily state who we truly are. In fact we can change, and I believe one of the best gifts bestowed on humanity is decision. Think about it. At any point in our lives, we can decide to feel sad or happy, we can decide whether to respond or react, and we can decide to stay still or move on. It is our choice. Unfortunately, we sometimes make our decisions based on: our past mistakes, our habits, and even more damaging, other people's opinions, experiences, or expectations. What is even more critical is sometimes, we just allow life to change us. Making decisions based on these kinds of influences will certainly keep you forever shackled. However, when you correctly make a decision straight from the heart, it will always feel right; this is what I call, absolute freedom.

Simply put, making the right changes requires a decision made from the heart.

What truly inspired me to create this book for you is the fact I used to be cantankerous, scornful, angry, and jealous but above all – I was depressed. Family members and friends often found it difficult to be around me, and at times I had difficulties with being in my own skin.

I used to blame all my "misfortunes" on other people when I was the one creating all of my problems. I had decided to be that person.

It was my fault. It was self-inflicted and I needed to make swift changes.

Much like you, my dear friends, I too am a work in progress. At times, I still struggle with certain things, yet I am OK with not being perfect, or for not "getting-things-right-the-first-time". I realize Rome wasn't built in a day and since the dawn of the Eternal City; Rome is still evolving – akin to all of humanity. When I began using positive affirmations, my life began to change. Soon thereafter, my friends and family began approaching me and would say, "I can't believe how much you've changed", or "You seem different."

The act of letting go when performed carefully and methodically can and will produce some of the most incredible results you can imagine. Letting go is a skill, and in order to become a master of this art form, you must: remain patient, be consistent, and overall, be incredibly grateful at all times.

Upon reading the affirmations provided, please emphasize on the wonderful feeling of gratitude. Brand the word gratitude upon the conscious mind and allow for the changes to unravel slowly. We all have something to be grateful for.

My goal for this book is to help change the consciousness of every reader. In order for this to happen, you must be made aware of what you are thinking about at a conscious level. For example, if you are feeling worried and you say:

"I am worried about…"

IMMEDIATELY cancel this thought and change it to something more positive like:

"I now visualize a perfect and healthy outcome."

Notice the affirmation is in the present tense? The reason is because we truly are this moment! We are not yesterday or tomorrow, we are right NOW.

Make the conscious decision to change. Change your mind. Focus on the outcome and focus on what you want. Always remember that what you want, wants you.

Let Go is designed for you.

Sincerely yours,

Antony S Scandale

antonyscandale.com

"To live continually in thoughts of ill will, cynicism, suspicion, and envy is to be confined to a self-made prison-hole. But to think well of all, to be cheerful with all, to patiently learn to find the good in all – such unselfish thoughts are the very portals of heaven; and to dwell day by day in thoughts of peace toward every creature will bring abounding peace to their possessor." **James Allen**

AFFIRMATION

"I live in a world of abundance.
I am abundance."

LET GO OF...

Lack

Reverse this now! You live in a world full of abundance. When you think about what you lack you WILL attract more of it. Understand, you attract what you want and what you don't want. Focus on what you want, focus on abundance.

AFFIRMATION

"I now exude love and respect towards everyone. We are equal."

LET GO OF...

Racism/Discrimination

We are created equal. Understand racism is taught and no one is born racist or discriminating. We have the choice and the strength to understand we are all equal.

AFFIRMATION

"I always show respect to myself and to others."

LET GO OF...

Disrespect

Being disrespectful is unattractive and rude. Build a better attitude by showing respect for those you know and meet. You never know what may come out of every meeting, such as a new job, or a long-lasting friendship. Be respectful and treat yourself with respect.

AFFIRMATION

"I now have enough, I am at peace."

LET GO OF...

Greed / Avarice

Greed drives dissatisfaction with what we already possess. We must take enough for ourselves and leave just as much for others to enjoy. Be grateful for what you have now and always.

AFFIRMATION

"I will always find a way to make my dreams come true."

LET GO OF...

Excuses

Making excuses will rob you of your dreams. Contented people never make excuses. In fact you take a step towards success the day you decide to let that habit go. Don't look for an excuse, find a way to make it happen. There are INFINITE ways to make your dreams come true.

AFFIRMATION

"I now have the energy, strength and ability to do more and to be more."

LET GO OF...

Laziness

Laziness never helps personal growth. Being lazy is the easiest way to cause atrophy in the body, the mind, and the soul. Do more in order to be more. Serve better to be better every day.

AFFIRMATION

"I now choose to be healthy and happy."

LET GO OF...

Gluttony

Overindulgence is never healthy, nor will it bring you happiness. Be aware of what you are consuming. Ask yourself, "Will this benefit me in the long run?" You have the strength and power to change.

AFFIRMATION

"I am so happy and grateful now to accept my gift."

MAGIC MOMENT

MAKE A WISH

Take a moment and take a deep breath.
Close your eyes and imagine exactly what it is
you want. Make it crystal clear and
KNOW your wish will come.

AFFIRMATION

"I now utilize my inner strength to get into action."

LET GO OF...

Procrastination

Do it! Why leave for tomorrow what you can do today? Make a decision to do whatever it is you want – however big or small. By making a decision, you allow opportunities, contacts and money to manifest. Yes, life is short but moments are shorter. Do it!

AFFIRMATION

"I remain humble at all times."

LET GO OF...

Vanity

It is great to love yourself; in fact it is encouraged. Yet vanity does not allow others to love you in return. Express more love to others.

AFFIRMATION

"I happily accept what will come.
I am at peace."

LET GO OF...

Assumptions

You invite delight into your life when you quit making assumptions. Assumptions are fables - end of story. Deleting assumptions from your life will let you live in the "now". Accept and enjoy what will come and learn from the outcome.

AFFIRMATION

"I now wait patiently knowing that
what I want is already here."

LET GO OF...

Impatience

Impatience, irritability, and restlessness not only damage your concentration but repel goals, wishes and dreams. Patience is sweet and serene. Remain calm, be patient and find tranquility.

AFFIRMATION

"I happily release the weight of past information and memories."

LET GO OF...

Old School Books/Texts/ Papers

De-clutter your room and office of old essays, drawings and text-books (the ones you forgot to give back to the school library). Sift through what you have and remove them accordingly.

AFFIRMATION

"I am so happy and grateful now to accept my gift."

MAGIC MOMENT

MAKE A WISH

Take a moment and take a deep breath.
Close your eyes and imagine exactly what it is
you want. Make it crystal clear and
KNOW your wish will come.

AFFIRMATION

"I now express love and peace
to those I meet."

LET GO OF...

Derogatory Language

Avoid the use of derogatory language. What you may think is true about someone doesn't make it so. Using derogatory language creates a low opinion of others and makes you look dishonest if what you said was absolutely false. Be mindful of what you think and say.

AFFIRMATION

"I am beautiful. I believe I am beautiful. I love who I am now and forever."

LET GO OF...

Beauty Standards

YOU ARE BEAUTIFUL! Never fall prey to what society believes is the way you should look, act, and dress. Be yourself! Love yourself! And love others because they in turn will love you.

AFFIRMATION

"I will now think once, twice and thrice before making a purchase."

LET GO OF...

Impulse Buying

Instant gratification is exactly that – it lasts a short while. Buy only what you need. When you spend money, be in a good mood, but cultivate the habit of saving. You'll thank yourself later.

AFFIRMATION

"I graciously send back all of which belongs to my ex. I am free."

LET GO OF...

Possessions from Ex's

Send it back to the rightful owner. When you return possessions to your ex, you are one step closer towards closure. Be gentle to them and always be gentle to yourself.

AFFIRMATION

"I love and accept we are equal."

LET GO OF...

Arrogance

Self-confidence is perfectly healthy; but being arrogant is simply fooling oneself to believe one is better than others. We are all created equal.

AFIRMATION

"I focus on my life and I am in control."

LET GO OF...

Meddling

You are in charge of your life, not the lives of others. Understand that your life is a 24-hour job. By sticking your nose into other people's business you are taking time and energy away from yourself. Strive for self-improvement. When you change your inner world, your outer world changes with you.

AFFIRMATION

"I now love and respect my body, mind and soul. I have loving support from my peers, now and always."

LET GO OF...

Drugs/Alcohol

Keep your mind clear and focused at all times. You have a beautiful body and a powerful mind; and people will always be there to help. Understand you are never alone. Reach out and ask for guidance. In the meantime, always see yourself healthy and happy.

AFFIRMATION

"I have a strong, healthy and loving attitude."

LET GO OF...

Bad Attitude

Having a bad attitude is NEVER positive, nor pleasing. A bad attitude is a sign of weakness in the body, mind and soul. Exude power, grace, self-control and self-respect for your world and for yourself.

AFFIRMATION

"I now express love and joy to myself and to others."

LET GO OF...

Resentment/Bitterness

What is bitter can be made sweet with a touch of love. Being resentful or bitter can and will cause physical ailments to your body. Release this emotional pain NOW. Express love and light to those who have wronged you but most importantly, forgive them and don't forget to forgive yourself.

AFFIRMATION

"I will hear and read positive messages."

LET GO OF...

Negative Music/Lyrics

Avoid this at all costs. By listening and reading negative content you are conditioning your mind to act and feel negative. Choose something positive to nurture your
mind, body and spirit.

AFFIRMATION

"I am calm, cool and collected.
I am at peace."

LET GO OF...

Stress

Stop for a moment and breathe through your nose and exhale through your mouth. Do this 3 times. Relax. Slow down the process. Understand, stress is always temporary – it has come to pass. Isn't that a lovely thought? When you are overwhelmed by stress, find somewhere quiet to meditate. The goal here is to center yourself before moving forward.

AFFIRMATION

"I now feel calm and I now focus on a solution. I am at peace."

LET GO OF...

Anger

Anger is a natural emotion. You don't have to bottle it in or explode every time you are angry. Write it out or perhaps, take a bat to a pillow. Understand there is a time and a place to express anger. Choose wisely. Once the emotions are out, FOCUS on a solution.

AFFIRMATION

"I now remain centered and
always in control."

LET GO OF...

Temptation

Mastering inner strength will allow you to eliminate temptation. It will permit you to stay focused on what is important. You are in control. Remain in control. Self-control is strength.

AFFIRMATION

"I am now flexible and eager to learn."

LET GO OF...

Stubbornness

This is a form of ignorance. Being stubborn hinders your ability to learn and grow. Take time to listen; try to be more flexible, more reasonable. Your life changes much faster when you let go of stubbornness.

AFFIRMATION

"I now have faith, trust, and courage to face the unknown."

LET GO OF...

FEAR

Fear is natural, but fear is WEAK. And it will make you weak if you don't summon your inner-strength and faith. Use fear as a stepping-stone toward success. What stops you is you. Take control and take ACTION. Action destroys fear immediately, so make the effort and push through. Do it with love, courage and strength. Remember: it is always better to try and fail than fail to try.

AFFIRMATION

"I am so happy and grateful now
to accept my gift."

MAGIC MOMENT

MAKE A WISH

Take a moment and take a deep breath. Close your eyes and imagine exactly what it is you want. Make it crystal clear and **KNOW** your wish will come.

AFFIRMATION

"I now find love and happiness in my life and I give support and love to everyone."

LET GO OF...

Jealousy

Jealousy places you on the other side of happiness. A jealous person is someone who is not happy with themselves and one who can never feel happy for other people's victories, possessions, or lifestyle. Learn to be grateful for yourself and for what you have first. Next, be genuinely happy for those you come in contact with – always!

AFFIRMATION

"I have faith and when I put faith first I never finish last."

LET GO OF...

Doubt

Doubt can sink a ship. It kills dreams and sets you up for unnecessary disaster. Show and express faith to yourself and others and say, "YES! It is possible".

AFFIRMATION

"I am willing to be teachable and
I will do my best to learn new things."

LET GO OF...

Ignorance

Ignorance never allows for knowledge to seep into your life. Ignorance closes the mind and acts as a mental block for learning. Do your best to learn. Ask many, many questions. We are here to teach and to learn.

AFFIRMATION

"I only focus on the 'know' and
I have faith the 'how' will come.
I am at peace."

LET GO OF...

HOW

Let go of HOW – even if you are desperate for answers. Understand the universe is in charge of the HOW. Your job is to KNOW and to have FAITH. Remember, the "how" is about the details you don't see just yet but they will come when you are ready. Focusing on the "how" will derail your spirit and make you frustrated. The "how" is none of your business.

AFFIRMATION

"I now visualize a healthy
and perfect outcome."

LET GO OF...

Worry

Let go of this now. Write out what is bothering you, and read it out loud. You will find what you are really worried about isn't so bad. Let the universe take care of the details.

AFFIRMATION

"I now and always listen to the facts and to my heart. I seek the truth."

LET GO OF...

Listening to Opinions of Others

Someone's opinion of you is none of your business. People will always create opinions about you and others. Listening and believing these opinions can potentially damage your life. Listen for facts! Never accept opinions as truth. Don't ever let someone's opinion about you become your reality.

AFFIRMATION

"I now speak positively about others."

LET GO OF...

Negative Talk of Others

Speak no ill will to any man or woman and when you hear someone speaking unfavorably about others, remove yourself from their presence. That's right, walk away! If you have something negative to say about others, write it out and burn it. However, the best thing to do is focus on the good qualities people have.

AFFIRMATION

"I now focus on improving
my inner world."

LET GO OF...

News Programs

This will surely give you some peace of mind. Often the News will broadcast stories that are depressing. That being said, turn off the News and work on yourself. You will always find second or third-hand News information from others. Try to avoid News Programs for one week.

AFFIRMATION

"I am in complete control of my mental faculties, and I base my decisions from my heart."

LET GO OF...

Pressure from Others

Who has to live with the consequences? Who dies with their experiences? That's right, YOU DO! So take control of you! Let go of others attempting to shape your world. Make your own decisions and make them from the heart.
You are in charge of YOU!

AFFIRMATION

"I am now conscious of the words I use to express my emotions."

LET GO OF...

Swearing

Words carry meaning. What you say is a direct reflection of your character. Choose your words carefully. Try for one day to stop swearing.

AFFIRMATION

"I now make time to be active."

LET GO OF...

Cable TV / Gaming

Dare yourself to reduce the hours you spend watching Cable TV and playing video games. Get up and go for a walk, a run, and join that team or dance. Get up and get active!

AFFIRMATION

"I now find inner peace."

LET GO OF...

Technology

Turn off the TV, radio, and the phone. Let go of technology for one hour or two. Read, meditate, speak to friends in person, plant a tree.
You get the idea.

AFFIRMATION

"I now surround myself with supportive and positive people."

LET GO OF...

Negative People

The negative people in your life could be your friends, family or spouses. Regardless of who they are, understand that people who are constantly negative towards you or others, are completely miserable inside. These people are the ones who need the most help. However, it is NOT your duty to change them. Avoid negative people at all costs, especially if they are people who are near and dear to your heart. This won't be easy because they will want you to join them in their "pity party". Don't give in. Find other people for support, people like-minded to you. When you leave negative people behind, be gentle to yourself and towards them. Negative people will either change with you or fall out of your life forever.

AFFIRMATION

"I am so happy and grateful now
to accept my gift."

MAGIC MOMENT

MAKE A WISH

Take a moment and take a deep breath. Close your eyes and imagine exactly what it is you want. Make it crystal clear and **KNOW** your wish will come.

AFFIRMATION

"I allow for my heart to produce thoughts of peace. I am perfect."

LET GO OF...

Negative Self-Talk

Never hurt yourself with words. You are worth it! Be kind to yourself. Love yourself always! Your subconscious mind is constantly listening and recording every word. Remain positive. Be positive. Keep the self-talk positive at all times!

AFFIRMATION

"I am grateful, thankful, and appreciative for all the things that make me happy."

LET GO OF...

Complaining

For one day, let go of complaints. No matter what it is – let it go! No one likes to hear a complainer. In fact everyone has their own problems to deal with and they would rather not hear about yours. If you are about to complain, stop and think of something to be thankful for. For example, family, siblings, or your health. This will surely raise your vibration up. You want to be happy, right?

AFFIRMATION

"I exchange the weight of pennies
for large bills."

LET GO OF...

Pennies

Do you really need all those extra pennies? If they all happen to be lucky or if you're a serious coin collector, by all means, keep them. Otherwise, why not exchange them for paper bills?

AFFIRMATION

"I am so happy and grateful now
to accept my gift."

MAGIC MOMENT

MAKE A WISH

Take a moment and take a deep breath. Close your eyes and imagine exactly what it is you want. Make it crystal clear and **KNOW** your wish will come.

AFFIRMATION

"I allow myself to find the gold in every situation. I choose love."

LET GO OF...

Hatred

Ask yourself what it is you hate and ask why you hate it. Hatred never allows love to enter your world. Try for just a day. Look at all the things you hate and find something positive about them. The goal is to look at things from a different perspective. Hatred breeds more hatred and love brings in more love. Choose to love.

AFFIRMATION

"I now have more room for the new to come in."

LET GO OF...

Loose Paper

Why keep loose paper of scribbling, receipts, and restaurant menus? Right now, get rid of loose paper from your desk. Empty your pockets. Clear out the menus attached to your fridge.

AFFIRMATION

"I now have clean underwear."

LET GO OF...

Underwear

Let's not get into the details of this. Just get rid of the old pairs of underwear. Buy some clean underwear every so often.

AFFIRMATION

"I now draw into my life positive and inspiring people."

LET GO OF...

Phone Numbers

Sift through your phone contacts and delete numbers you don't have use for. Of course keep your parents', or best friend's number in there.

AFFIRMATION

"I now have a pair of brand new shoes."

LET GO OF...

Shoes

Chances are your feet won't grow any larger unless you are expecting another growth spurt. Regardless, if they smell, have holes in them, or haven't been used in over
12 months – kick them out.

AFFIRMATION

"I now have a new toothbrush."

LET GO OF...

Toothbrush

Is it worn down to the plastic? Do the bristles fan out like a plant? Three to four months after delicate enamel polishing, it will be wise to replace the old canine scrubber.

AFFIRMATION

"I now expose my true self to the world."

LET GO OF...

Hats

Reduce the amount of hats you have at home. If you have an overabundance of hats consider giving them away. Go one week without wearing a hat – the world wants to see your face.

AFFIRMATION

"I now happily give the opportunity to someone who is willing to play this instrument."

LET GO OF...

Instruments

An instrument needs to be played on a daily basis. Fill your world with music. Otherwise, donate your instrument to someone who will love to learn how to play.

AFFIRMATION

"I release the clutter of old movies and audiotapes."

LET GO OF...

Audio/Visual

Whether they are audiotapes, VHS, Beta, or DVD's, get rid of them if you don't use them often. Trade them in or sell them for some extra cash.

AFFIRMATION

"I am so happy and grateful now
to accept my gift."

MAGIC MOMENT

MAKE A WISH

Take a moment and take a deep breath. Close your eyes and imagine exactly what it is you want. Make it crystal clear and **KNOW** your wish will come.

AFFIRMATION

"I now create new and better habits."

LET GO OF...

Bad Habit

We can all learn from this. Choose one bad habit and stop doing it for 24 hours. If you can make it past 24 hours, make it 48 hours. The habit will go away IF you are consistent. Remember, habits are paradigms – but you have the ability to change them.

AFFIRMATION

"I now have an active, happy and healthy lifestyle."

LET GO OF...

Pills/Medications

Check the expiry dates and send the meds back to the pharmacist for proper disposal. If you are using pills and medications, understand and believe you CAN live a healthy life by eating properly and by being active, joyful, and appreciative.

AFFIRMATION

"I now have new clothing and I look and feel great!"

LET GO OF...

Clothing

Small, smelly, and stained clothing must be tossed. Don't hesitate to downsize your closet right away. Get rid of 5 items and look forward to a new snappy ensemble.

AFFIRMATION

"I now provide sporting opportunities to those who want it."

LET GO OF...

Sporting Equipment

Get rid of the snowboard. Sell the lacrosse stick. Give the deflated football the punt out of your life. Otherwise, be charitable and find someone who will put the equipment to immediate use.

AFFIRMATION

"I am highly skilled and ready for a new challenge."

LET GO OF...

Old Resumes

You don't really need those old resumes do you? Of course not. Why not revamp your resume? Make it look clean, spice it up, and add more experiences and skills to the paper.

AFFIRMATION

"I now have new make-up."
"I now have new razors."

LET GO OF...

Make-Up/Razors

Old makeup has been known to house bacteria and can potentially do harmful things to your skin, while old razors (you too guys) can cause rashes on your face and other parts of your body.

AFFIRMATION

"I now have new clean pairs of socks."

LET GO OF...

Old Socks

So someone invites you over to their house and after arriving, you take off your shoes. It is then you realize your big toe decides to say hello to your host. Yeah, no brainer. Toss out those frayed, worn out socks before your toes make an unexpected visit.

AFFIRMATION

"I now have a clean home environment."

LET GO OF...

Garbage

This is your chance to be shrewd. Letting go is an art. Sometimes you just have to bite the bullet and get rid of things. Sure, take out the garbage, but while you are at it, see what else you can let go of.

AFFIRMATION

"I now have perfect writing utensils."

LET GO OF...

Pens/Pencils

Pen out of ink or won't work? Pencil too small to hold? Perhaps you have an overabundance of pens and pencils? Keep what works and throw out the rest, or donate them to a school or a student. Perhaps take them back to the office or the bank. I won't tell.

AFFIRMATION

"I look forward to bigger and better experiences."

LET GO OF...

Journals

Having a journal is a great idea. However, if you plan on getting rid of ancient memories and emotions attached to a journal, then make the decision to throw it away or burn it in a metal bucket. Read a few passages, reminisce, laugh, cry and then let go of it forever. Next, take a good look at yourself. Realize you have come this far, and you are bigger and better because of those experiences.

AFFIRMATION

"I now focus on my personal growth and life."

LET GO OF...

Gossip

Gossip is POISON! Don't give into the nasty conversation. Make it a habit to never engage in gossip; and if you hear something "juicy", walk away. Remember, the information you hear will not benefit your life or your wallet. For 24 hours try to avoid spreading and listening to gossip. Your mind will thank you.

AFFIRMATION

"I now attract information which will
benefit my life and the
lives of others."

LET GO OF...

Books/Magazines

Return them to the library or hand them back to the person who lent them to you.

AFFIRMATION

"I now move forward."

LET GO OF...

Photos of Your Ex

Challenge yourself to let go of photographs of your ex. Understand what you shared with each other was fun, but now it's time to move on. Be gentle about your thoughts toward them when you reflect on the past. Thank them in spirit, let go and look forward. If there are any photos that could be used for "blackmail", definitely get rid of them. Be the better person. Let go and move on.

AFFIRMATION

"I now have room for better things."

LET GO OF...

Empty Bottles/Cans

Clean out your garage, cupboards and kitchen of those empty bottles. Recycle for cash or give the bottles to a little league team to help their fundraising. Think green.

AFFIRMATION

"I graciously give away toys to the needy."

LET GO OF...

Toys

Find a charity. Better yet, find a child or two who would LOVE to own some of your toys. Watch their faces afterwards; you'll be glad you did.

AFFIRMATION

"I now choose to eat healthy foods."

LET GO OF...

Junk Food

Overconsuming junk food can decrease growth and development in toddlers and teens. It can also cause weight gain, dental problems, and poor concentration. When the mind is pure with good thoughts, the body will no longer need impure food. Build a repulsion for junk food.

AFFIRMATION

"I now have fresh batteries."

LET GO OF...

Dead Batteries

Dead or dying batteries will not keep things going and going. You can recycle your batteries properly. Look in your area and see if there is a Battery Disposal place.

AFFIRMATION

"I now keep my thoughts peaceful, beautiful, and joyful."

LET GO OF...

Negative Thoughts

If you have a negative thought brewing, CANCEL IT RIGHT AWAY! Go a full day monitoring your thoughts and replace them with positive ones. Make this a habit. Do your best to keep your mind happy, joyful and always POSITIVE.

AFFIRMATION

"I release the things which no longer serve me."

LET GO OF...

Broken Things

Unless you're handy or have the absolute know-how and motivation to fix something, then fix it. Otherwise do yourself a big favor and let go of it. TOSS IT NOW. You are only holding on to dead energy.

AFFIRMATION

"I am so happy and grateful now
to accept my gift."

MAGIC MOMENT

MAKE A WISH

Take a moment and take a deep breath. Close your eyes and imagine exactly what it is you want. Make it crystal clear and **KNOW** your wish will come.

AFFIRMATION

"I let go of electronics which no longer serve me."

LET GO OF...

Outdated Electronics

Is your CD player busted? The record player won't spin anymore? Your 8-track player needs to be put into a museum? Yes? Then let go and say good-bye.

AFFIRMATION

"I now receive new and useful information."

LET GO OF...

Old Newspapers/Magazines

Think of it this way: It's all OLD NEWS. Why dwell in the past of old information? Give them away or recycle them. Here's a tip: create a vision board, a collage of things you want to see come into your life, by using clippings from newspapers and magazines.

AFFIRMATION

"I now have space for new memories."

LET GO OF...

Photos

This may be tough, but do you really need to keep every single photo or "selfie"? Downsize your hard drive, your phone and photo albums by eliminating photos that are doubles, faded, out of focus, or unappealing.

AFFIRMATION

"My inbox is now clean and ready to receive new and exciting information."

LET GO OF...

Delete E-mail

Give your inbox and your mind a rest. Delete all e-mails that are no longer pertinent to your life. Otherwise, file them for later use if they happen to be important. Make it a habit to clean out your e-mail once every two weeks.

AFFIRMATION

"I now speak the truth, I am free."

LET GO OF...

Lying

You only hurt and deceive yourself when you lie.
From now on, believe and understand
the truth will set you free.

NOTES

NOTES

NOTES

www.ingramcontent.com/pod-product-compliance
Lightning Source LLC
Chambersburg PA
CBHW071004160426
43193CB00012B/1906